UNMASKING THE POWER WITHIN

UNMASKING THE POWER WITHIN

MASTERING THE 5 FORCES OF SELF-AWARENESS FOR EXTRAORDINARY LEADERSHIP

DR EMMANUEL ENI
AMADI

PhD, MBA, PGDip., MSc, B.Pharm.

Copyright ©2023 – Dr Emmanuel Eni Amadi.

UNMASKING THE POWER WITHIN: Mastering The 5 Forces of Self-Awareness For Extraordinary Leadership
ISBN: 978-1-7398778-2-8 (Paperback)
First Published in the United Kingdom by
Amadi Global Publishing (AGP), an imprint of
AMADI GLOBAL LEADERSHIP ACADEMY LTD
The Global Centre, GLASGOW, SCOTLAND, UNITED KINGDOM
https://www.amadiglobal.co.uk/publishing
E-mail: info@amadiglobal.co.uk

Unless otherwise indicated, Scripture quotations in this book are from the Holy Bible, New International Version (NIV, Anglicised edition) Copyright ©1979, 1984, 2011 by Biblica (formerly International Bible Society. Use by permission of Holder & Stoughton Publishers, A Hachette UK Company. All rights reserved.

This book is protected by copyright laws of the United Kingdom. Any unauthorised copying, reproduction or storage of this book, in any form, is prohibited without written permission from the author. Written permission is required for any commercial copying or storage of this book in electronic formats. Short quotations in critical articles and reviews are allowed without seeking approval. Dr Emmanuel Eni Amadi, the author, has the exclusive copyright to this book, and his moral right has been asserted. **Amadi Global Publishing (AGP),** functions only as a publisher of this book. As a result, the ultimate design, book contents, editorial, precision, and views expressed or implied in this work are those of the author.

British Library Cataloguing in Publication Data
A catalogue record for this book is available from the British Library.
Paperback ISBN: 978-1-7398778-2-8; 1. Personal Transformation. 2. Business & Money – Leadership & Management. 3. Self-Help.

About Amadi Global Publishing (AGP)
Amadi Global Publishing is an imprint of Amadi Global Leadership Academy Ltd, a UK Company Registered in Edinburgh, Scotland, UK.
Book Cover Design, editing, proofreading, and formatting by Dr E E Amadi.

Disclaimer

Please carefully review the following disclaimer before proceeding to ensure that you fully understand the content and purpose of the book.

1. General Information:

'Unmasking The Power Within' is a work of fiction. Any resemblance to actual persons, living or dead, or events is purely coincidental. The characters, names, places, and incidents portrayed in this book are either the product of the author's imagination or are used fictitiously. It is essential to mention that any similarity to real-life individuals, organizations or locations is entirely unintentional. Where real names have been used, consent had been obtained.

2. Disclaimer of Liability:

This book's author and publisher have made every effort to ensure the accuracy of the information. They disclaim any liability for damages, losses, or consequences resulting from using or interpreting this information, but assume no responsibility for errors, inaccuracies, or omissions.

3. Content Warning:

Topics in this book may be sensitive or controversial. The author acknowledges that this book may only be appropriate for some readers. Reader discretion is advised. It is recommended that individuals under 18 or those sensitive to its content seek guidance from a responsible adult before engaging with it.

4. Personal Interpretation:

In this book, the author expresses his opinion and does not necessarily represent the publisher's position. The author intends to entertain and provoke thought, but readers should form their own opinions and interpretations of the content within this book.

5. External Links:

Several references to external websites, products, or services may be found in this book. The author and publisher are not responsible for external resources' content, accuracy, or availability. Readers who choose to access such links do so at their own risk.

Dr Emmanuel Eni Amadi (PhD MBA) is available for consultation and speaking engagements on the topics discussed in this book, whether with government bodies, institutions, churches, or individual situations.

~ 27 August 2023

Contents

Dedication IX

Introduction 1

1. The Concept of "Power" in Leadership 7
2. The Power of Purpose in Leadership 23
3. The Power of Identity in Leadership 37
4. The Power of INSIGHT in Leadership 47
5. The Power of Reputation in Leadership 57
6. The Power of IMAGE vs BRAND in Leadership 71

Conclusion: 87

About the Author 91

Books Published by the Author 93

How to Contact Us 95

Dedication

This book is dedicated to my wife,
Mrs Ewa (Eva) Amadi
(n*ee Klosowska*)
She has encouraged me to pursue my dreams of helping others live better – whether in healthcare or in my leadership training programmes.
Wow!
We celebrated our
15th Wedding anniversary on 28 July 2023.
We thank God for our lives
– in good times and in bad times.
We thank Him for keeping us together
during our most challenging moments.

Introduction

Mastering effective leadership is a challenging journey comparable to navigating through Japan's winding "Iroha-Zaka" Road, complete with 48 hairpin curves, valleys, and mountains. It has its uncertainties, privileges, and hopes. Effective leadership requires a sharp understanding of external factors and internal self-discovery. "Unmasking the Power Within: Mastering The 5 Forces of Self-Awareness For Extraordinary Leadership" is an indispensable tool for individuals who aspire to impact their leadership roles significantly.

In contemporary society, influential figures such as celebrities, politicians, and social media personalities hold significant sway over people's decisions. They advocate for various causes, such as healthy lifestyles, a drug-free society, and eco-consciousness, which can place considerable pressure on individuals to conform to societal norms. This pressure is evident in the struggles of newlyweds to purchase a home or students who need help to gain admission to their preferred universities.

The pressure to conform is not limited to individuals but entire industries that strive to mould outcomes according to their preferences, with medical professionals seeking Power over diseases and financial institutions attempting to manage poverty. Meanwhile, individuals of faith yearn for miraculous events that validate their connection to the divine or supernatural deity.

Throughout history, humanity has relentlessly pursued Power and dominion, driven to exert control over its surroundings. In my experience as a leader in my field and a mentor to senior managers, I have learnt that being a leader entails skillfully navigating challenging circumstances.

In recent years, the focus has shifted from Emotional Intelligence (EQ) to Artificial Intelligence (AI). Several industries utilise AI, including self-driving automobiles and heart surgery. However, despite these external power pursuits, it is essential to note that genuine leadership or the untapped natural Power, which is the ability to inspire and drive change by attracting followership, lies dormant within each individual and remains critical. That Power is the secret ingredient that propels leaders towards greatness and turns cowards into agents of change.

That Power is Self-Awareness or Consciousness – the profound understanding and acceptance of one's strengths, weaknesses, emotions, motives, and motivations.

Self-awareness involves being CONSCIOUS of one's 'inter-and-intrapersonal' dynamics: leadership style, communication patterns, and knowledge of the IMPACT one's emotions, actions, and reactions have on others. It's also about how one's behaviour aligns with one's values and goals. In business, Self-awareness involves being 'mindful' of the organization's value proposition, missions and visions, culture, reputation, and Image.

With this knowledge harvested from within, every challenge becomes a theatre to practice your new skills. Every failure becomes a leadership lesson. And every threat or crisis becomes a unique opportunity to multiply and grow.

This book, "Unmasking the Power Within," seeks to uncover and unleash your hidden potential. It transcends the boundaries of specific industries and focuses on the immense Power that resides within your very being. By delving into the depths of Self-Awareness, we will explore "The 5 POWERFUL FORCES" or "The 5 PILLARS" of Self-Awareness that can transform your leadership abilities and bring about meaningful change.

BOOK CHAPTERS AND DIVISION

This book is divided into SIX Chapters:

Chapter 1: The Concept of POWER in Leadership:

This Chapter sets the stage by unravelling the enigma of Power itself. You will discover how to harness and wield Power to elevate your leadership to unprecedented heights. Let go of outdated concepts of POWER and embrace a new definition of POWER built on self-awareness and authentic connection. This Chapter ends with exercise categories with ten practical sub-exercises to evaluate your understanding of 'The Concept of Power in Leadership.'

Next is Chapter 2: The Power of PURPOSE in Leadership:

This Chapter delves into the breathtaking Power of Purpose. Unleash the driving force that propels visionary leaders toward greatness. With Dr Emmanuel Amadi's guidance, you'll uncover your true-life Purpose, align it with your leadership ambitions, and launch yourself on a transformative journey to success and fulfilment. Like the previous Chapter, Chapter 2 ends with practical exercises to assess what you've studied.

Moving forward, you will explore **Chapter 3 - The POWER of IDENTITY in Leadership,**" which takes you on an exploration of the Power of identity. Learn the five steps to cultivate your leadership Identity, the unwavering sense of self rooted in your core values and beliefs. Discover how aligning your personal and professional identities equips you to lead with integrity, validity, and unshakeable conviction. This Chapter ends with five engaging exercises to evaluate your understanding.

As your mastery unfolds to the next higher level, Dr Amadi guides you through **Chapter 4** to reveal the profound **"Power of INSIGHT in Leadership."** You will gain invaluable techniques to transform your world from the "unseen" to the "seen world." Become a leader who understands human behaviour's intricacies and effectively navigates any challenge. Because 'the taste of the pudding is in the eating', this Chapter ends with five powerful exercises to test your understanding.

As you reach **Chapter 5: The Power of REPUTATION in Leadership**, it's time to unlock the Power of Reputation. Dr Amadi uses an anecdotal story and lessons from reputable business leaders and a political leader to explore how building your reputation could endure through impact, leaving behind a valuable legacy. With 11-proven steps for creating a leadership reputation, you will build endearing Trust, foster collaboration, and consistently deliver exceptional value-driven results that resonate far beyond your time as a leader.

This Chapter ends with seven practical exercises. From defining your leadership values to conflict resolution exercises, you will develop a leadership reputation in the eyes of your target audience.

Finally, in Chapter 6, you will enter the spotlight and embrace **The POWER of IMAGE vs BRAND** in Leadership. Here, Dr Amadi discusses the concept of "Image" with theology, business, and leadership. You will understand the ten proven strategies anyone can adopt to establish themselves as a trusted authority in their field of discipline, job, or social class, leveraging their influence to inspire others and advance their leadership journey.

Throughout this book, **"Unmasking the Power Within,"** we will unlock your hidden potential by exploring each of the FIVE Powerful Forces in Self-Awareness. By embarking upon this journey of self-discovery and unearthing your true Power, you will uncover the keys to becoming a more self-aware, influential, and impactful leader.

My dear readers, if you are ready to embark on this transformative journey towards becoming more self-aware and influential leaders in your area of specialisation or work, let us begin this exploration of the FIVE Powerful Forces that lie within us and eagerly await your unmasking.

Chapter One

The Concept of "Power" in Leadership

Power comes in various forms and contexts. When people hear about "Power," what comes to mind is "Political Power". Everyone has the same inherent Power and influence hidden inside them, but our social-cultural and 'belief systems' have conditioned our minds to think that POWER and Influence belong to a particular group.

In your current job, your manager has Power or authority over junior employees based on their position. They use this authority to control your behaviour at the workplace, including the hours you work per week. When tired of you, they can box you into the corner of resignation, offering few slots to frustrate your Power financially and render you powerless. The manager in this situation has considerable Power: Power is given based on their position but has yet to earn it. Someone with this kind of Power can abuse their authority if it's unchecked.

In other dimensions of Power, a notable example is the Power to overcome life-threatening events. Such Powers include driving a Toyota car this year and upgrading to the newer Range Rover or Rolls-Royce Phantom next year. Being single this year to upgrading to the "Just Married" level next year," and from being unemployed for the past four years to landing your first Executive job this year. These are dominion powers.

In the context of leadership, "Power" refers to the ability to influence and make decisions that affect others to achieve specific, desired goals or outcomes. It involves directing or indirectly controlling others' actions, processes, and resources with or without resistance.

Therefore, Power in leadership is the ability to initiate changes in your present circumstances that shift you from where you are in your current life circumstances (poor lifestyle) to the next highest level of abundance (affluent lifestyle) and freedom you desire.

Why Do People Seek POWER?

Individuals seek leadership positions to gain Power and control to address unfavourable circumstances in communities or organisations. In the following paragraphs, I will provide the five primary reasons why people seek Power:

(1) Influence and Control

One of the core reasons people seek Power in leadership is to have the ability to influence and control others. Power allows individuals to make decisions and direct others towards achieving specific objectives.

(2) Prestige and status

Power often brings prestige and status. Being in a leadership position can elevate an individual's social ranking and provide them with recognition and respect from others.

(3) Achievement and Success

A few individuals seek Power in leadership as a manifestation of their desire for achievement and success. Holding a position of Power in society allows such individuals to take charge, set goals, and drive their teams or organisations towards success.

(4) Personal development and growth

Leadership positions allow individuals to develop and grow personally. Taking on challenging responsibilities and overcoming obstacles can enhance problem-solving, decision-making, and interpersonal communication skills, leading to personal growth.

(5) To Make a Difference

Many people seek Power in leadership because they want to impact their environment or society positively. Holding a position of Power enables individuals to influence and implement changes that can shape the future and bring about positive outcomes for others.

Sources of Power in Leadership

While there are hundreds of power sources in leadership, I would narrow them down to NINE from different regions worldwide.

#1: Charismatic Power

Leaders with a natural charm and persuasive personality can inspire and motivate followers. In the United Kingdom, the two former Prime Ministers - Winston Churchill (1940-1945 and 1951-1955) and Margaret Thatcher (1970-1990) – were known for their charismatic Power that led their political parties to win elections.

#2: Expert Power

Leaders with extensive knowledge and expertise in a particular field wield Power by being regarded as experts. Renowned scientists, intellectuals, or industry leaders can represent this type of Power. People who fall into this category include Tim Cook (Apple), Mark Zuckerberg and Sheryl Sandberg (Facebook), Elon Musk (Tesla, SpaceX, and X (Twitter), and many more names in the tech industry.

#3: Legitimate Power

Leaders who hold formal positions of authority, like elected officials or government representatives, have Power given to them by the system and society.

#4: Reward Power

Leaders who can reward and provide incentives to others, such as managers who control salary raises or bonuses, can influence and motivate their subordinates.

#5: Traditional Power

In some African countries, like the IGBO tribe in Eastern Nigeria, in the former Republic of Biafra, leadership power is inherited or passed down through traditional and cultural systems, including tribal chiefs or kings.

#6: Coercive Power

There are many words associated with 'coercion.' They include force, bullying, intimidation, and violence. Autocratic and authoritarian leaders fall into this category. Leaders in this category use intimation, punishment or threats to enforce their authority over people under their control. Historical examples include dictators like Adolf Hitler of Germany and Benito Mussolini of Italy, known as the founder of fascism. They used fear and force to control their nations. Vladimir Putin of Russia may fall into this category, too.

Magnus Linden, a senior psychology lecturer at Lund University, and his co-author George Wilkes assert in their book "The Psychology Behind Destructive Leadership" that Putin's invasion of Ukraine in 2022 exposes his autocratic leadership style, which relies on coercive forces and repressive social controls to achieve his political goals.[1]

#7: Informational Power

A leader who strategically uses critical information to influence decisions and others belongs to this class. Intelligence agency directors such as the Secret Intelligence Service (SIS or MI6), the Security Service (MI5), the Government Communications Headquarters (GCHQ) in the UK or the US's Federal Bureau of Investigation (FBI) or top National Security Advisers possess his kind of Power.

#8: Hierarchical Power

In several Asian cultures, leaders who hold higher positions within the traditional social hierarchy or maintain leadership in family-based businesses wield significant Power.

#9: Inspirational Power

I had chosen to write on 'Inspirational Power' last to give me enough room to express my deep connection with the Power of inspiration that lies with us from millions of people worldwide. People in this group come from across all continents and the strata of our economy.

In the continent of Africa, where I was born, great leaders who have led liberation movements or fought for political freedom for their countries fall into this group. These include the likes of Julius Nyerere (Tanzania) and Nelson Mandela (South Africa). These two individuals gained Power through their inspiring ideas and commitment to the well-being of their people.

Nigeria, located in West Africa, proudly boasts of visionary leaders hailing from the Yoruba and Biafran Nations. When writing this paragraph on 13 August 2023, notable freedom fighters have inspired millions of followers through inspiration.

In Western Nigeria is Chief Sunday Adeniyi Adeyemo, known as Sunday Igboho, who's fighting for the independence of the Yoruba Nation. In Eastern Nigeria, comprising the former Citizens of the Republic of Biafra (1967-1970) are powerful and influential leaders in the likes of Mazi Nnamdi Kanu (MNK)[2] - a British Citizen and the leader of the Indigenous People of Biafra (IPOB) and his Finnish-based disciple, Simon Ekpa - an international lawyer, a Finnish Citizen and Politician. Although born in Nigeria, both freedom fighters, MNK and Ekpa, had since renounced their Nigerian Citizenship. They, too, are fighting peacefully to restore the Republic of Biafra.

Until now, MNK is still languishing in the Department of State Services (DSS) custody in Abuja, Nigeria, after being extraordinarily renditioned from Kenya. MNK and Ekpa have led the global Biafran movement through non-violent protests and the 'sit-at-home' mass civil disobedience.

India's Mahatma Gandhi first used this strategy of mass civil disobedience or satyagraha in 1906 against the South African Transvaal regime to protest the restriction of India's rights. On his return to India, he deployed the same strategy successfully in protest against British oppression, leading to Indian independence in 1947. IPOB has successfully utilised the same sit-at-home civil disobedience strategy with historic results.

In Asia, in addition to Mahatma Gandhi, we also have the like of Dalai Lama, who has demonstrated wisdom and spiritual guidance to command millions of followers worldwide through peaceful ideologies.

While the above nine sources of Power exist, it is vital to note that Power in leadership can be derived from multiple sources simultaneously, and leaders may employ different forms of Power to address specific situations or challenges at other times.

"Leadership is about harnessing and wielding Power to bring about positive changes in our society, locally and globally."

Dr Emmanuel Eni Amadi

Harnessing and Wielding Power in Leadership

Leadership is not about the accumulation of Power for personal gain. Instead, leadership is about "harnessing" and "wielding" Power to bring about positive changes in our society, locally and globally.

In this section, we will explore how leaders from different regions, specifically the UK, USA, India, and Africa, have harnessed their Power in leadership to elevate themselves and their communities to unprecedented heights. Through their inspiring examples, we will understand how these leaders championed causes closer to the hearts of their people and future generations.

1. Power as Visionary

In the United States, Martin Luther King Jr[3] was a problem solver. King fought against racial discrimination and advocated for civil rights for African-Americans in the US.

By painting a vision of a future where equality prevailed, King harnessed his Power as a leader to empower individuals, promote peaceful protests, and bring about lasting change.

Mahatma Gandhi was also a problem solved in India: Gandhi led India's struggle for independence from British rule, championing non-violent resistance against oppression.

Gandhi's Power as a leader stemmed from his ability to envision a free India, inspiring millions to join the independence movement through non-violent protests, civil disobedience, and passive resistance.

In South Africa, Nelson Mandela solved the problem of apartheid. Mandela fought against apartheid in South Africa, advocating for equality and reconciliation.

He harnessed his Power as a visionary leader by envisioning a future free from racial discrimination, leading the anti-apartheid movement, and eventually becoming the country's first black President.

2. Power of Empathy and Compassion

Emmeline Pankhurst is unequivocally renowned for her unparalleled problem-solving abilities in the United Kingdom. She fearlessly spearheaded the women's suffrage movement, relentlessly fighting for their right 'to vote' and 'be voted for' in general elections and referendums. Pankhurst deeply understood women's hardships and led the Suffragette Movement with unyielding determination, forcefully demanding equality through peaceful demonstrations and civil disobedience.

Franklin D. Roosevelt (the 32 US President) was the people's problem solver in the US. Roosevelt tackled the Great Depression and guided the United States through World War II. His Power as a leader came from his compassionate approach. He implemented social programs through his New Deal policies, including job creation and economic reforms, to uplift Americans during hardship.

India is not lagging when it comes to the Power of empathy and compassion. Mother Teresa devoted her life in India to serving the impoverished and marginalised communities, creating charitable organisations and hospices that have since expanded globally. Her unwavering compassion and ceaseless actions have left an enduring humanitarian impact.

Africa is full of individuals with both empathy and compassion. Wangari Maathai (1940-2011) of Kenya is a notable figure and a problem solver. Maathai addressed deforestation and environmental degradation while advocating for democracy and human rights in Kenya.

Her leadership power stemmed from her compassion for both people and the environment. She led the Green Belt Movement, encouraging women to plant trees, empowering communities and promoting sustainable development.

Conclusion

As a leader, one must profoundly comprehend one's responsibilities towards the greater good of the people and the nation to wield Power effectively. This segment highlights the experiences of leaders from various regions, including the United Kingdom, United States, India, and Africa, who have successfully harnessed their Power to support causes that strike a chord with the masses and pave the way for a brighter future for generations. A visionary, empathetic, and compassionate leader can propel their organisation to unparalleled heights and leave a lasting impact on their society and communities.

Chapter 1 Exercises:
The Concept of "Power" in Leadership

Exercise 1: Power Exploration

(1a) Reflect on the different forms of Power you have studied in this Chapter.

In your notebook, draw two columns: "Types of Power" on the left and the "Examples" on the right. Identify examples of each from your personal or professional life.

(1b) Discuss with a partner or a small group how power dynamics influence leadership within your organisation or team.

Exercise 2: Power Analysis

(2a) Analyse a case study or a real-world example of a leader and identify the sources of Power they possess.

(2b) Reflect on how the leader's Power impacts their effectiveness and team dynamics.

Exercise 3: Power Inventory

(3a) Create a list of your sources of Power as a leader, such as expertise, relationships, or access to resources.

(3b) Assess how effectively you utilise each power source to influence and lead others.

Exercise 4: Power Mapping

(4a) Map out the power dynamics within your organisation or team by identifying key individuals and their sources of Power.

(4b) Consider how these power dynamics influence decision-making and communication within the group.

Exercise 5: Power Sharing

(5a) Discuss and develop strategies for sharing Power with others in a leadership role.

(5b) Identify opportunities to delegate responsibility and empower team members to enhance collaboration and engagement.

---

1. Linden, Magnus, Wilkes, George R. (2022) Putin: The psychology behind his destructive leadership – and how best to tackle it according to science: Website: https://theconversation.com/putin-the-psychology-behind-his-destructive-leadership-and-how-best-to-tackle-it-according-to-science-179823 [Date accessed: 30 July 2023].

2. Awoyemi, A., & Okuande, O. (2020). The Politics of Biafran Separatism in Nigeria: Spikes and Falls in the Intensity of the Agitatio. Africa Policy Journal, 58.

3. Lydia Dishman (01-21-2019), Senior Editor at Fastcompany.com. Source: https://www.fastcompany.com/90936932/how-to-make-friends-at-work-your-first-week-on-the-job

Chapter Two

The Power of Purpose in Leadership

Igniting Your Inner Fire

"Purpose" is often associated with 'intention', 'meaning', 'direction,' 'function', 'reason,' 'motive', or 'motivation.' "Purpose" is the reason in the mind of every manufacturer of a product – the core solutions that the development, business, or employees are 'assigned' or 'designed' to accomplish in their lifetime. But how do you define this important word called "Purpose"? And how do you find the Purpose of a thing, product or person?

Thank you for reading this book up to this Chapter. But I have some questions to ask you. I will urge you to pause for a minute to ask yourself these three critical questions:

(1) Why was I born? (answers the question of Purpose).

(3) Why am I here - in my present circumstances?

(4) What shall I do to fulfil my Purpose? (answers the question of taking action).

Could your answers be like those of others, like, "*I was born to work hard, pay bills, get married, get old, retire, and gradually fade into oblivion*?" I believe life is more valuable and meaningful than just working hard at someone's job to pay bills, getting old, and then vanishing out of memory through death.

In his leadership book, "In Pursuit of Purpose", Dr. Myles Munroe (1992) reveals the answers in the following statements: *"The nature of something is a powerful clue to its purpose and potential."* Why? Because *"The Creator never requires anything of His creations that He didn't already build into them."* That means everyone is born with a purpose in mind before conception. All things have a sense of Purpose. None is a mere source of amusement.

The apple tree in the garden grows for a purpose: to yield good fruits in its season. 'Purpose' wakes you like these men on a building site in the morning. One early morning, as I looked through the window from our Scottish home, I saw ten young men working on a new property development a few walking distances away. These men arrived at the building site as early as 6 AM with one Purpose in their minds: to build high-quality homes for the next generation. That is Purpose.

Eight Steps To Know When 'Purpose' Flies Around You

Seeing 'Purpose' in black and white or 3-D format is often challenging. Below are the eight steps to help you recognise when Purpose presents itself so that you live a life of fulfilment.

1) ALIGNMENT:

'Purpose' is the alignment of YOUR actions, wills, and intents to the original reason you exist and the original reason you hold your current job title. Purpose answers the "WHY question": Why does your business exist? Why did you buy a new smartphone or a new wristwatch?

2) STRIVING:

'Purpose' is about YOU striving to fulfil your responsibilities in alignment with the maker's mind - whether in a product, actions, or humans.

3) RIGHT vs GOOD:

Purpose is about YOU doing the right things consistently (righteousness) and with the right mindset.

4) FEELING:

When you achieve your function through lawful adherence to the natural laws (Ts & Cs) set by the maker, rather than pursuing personal ambition outside the 'real purpose', you cannot help but feel fulfilled.

5) MAGNETIC FORCE:

"Purpose" is the number one magnetic force that propels leaders forward, stirring their souls and inspiring them to take action - even in challenging times.

6) THE YEAST IN A DOUGH:

The critical driving factor (CDF) buried inside every 'purpose' enables leaders to overcome obstacles and guide them through personal and professional journeys.

7) LIFEBLOOD:

"Purpose" infuses your work with meaning, and constantly fuels your desire to make a difference.

8) IMPACT:

Individuals who clearly understand their 'Purpose' in life possess more potential for impact than those who have fallen prey to confusion, trial and error, and abuse of authority.

PURPOSE IN ACTION:
John Smith – The Man With Purpose

The inspiration behind the book sub-heading, 'Purpose in Action: John Smith – The Man With Purpose,' came from a man I know in his mid-50s who wholeheartedly devoted himself to fulfilling the wants and needs of others.

In the quiet town of Robroyston, located in the heart of Glasgow's countryside, there is a unique street closer to the Motorway/superhighway where I live with my wife and children. This charming cul-de-sac is home to only eight exquisite houses, four on each side of the road.

We think that God visits Robroyston to watch over the inhabitants. My family and I were fortunate to witness a spectacular sight one evening. We saw what appeared to be a blazing barbecue fire that looked like a volcanic eruption from the hills nearby. There was no smoke except hot-dazzling clouds of fire piercing their fingers through the clear clouds. Luckily, my wife had the mind to capture the entire scene on video.

One dark Spring evening, the town rested under a thick blanket of dark clouds as the Sun covered itself with dark blankets to form the night and let the inhabitants have a quality night's sleep. There was a sudden power outage past midnight for the first time since we moved into the area. This unexpected incident plunged our home into abysmal darkness.

My wife and I woke up in darkness and stumbled around the house. We checked every room, lounge and kitchen to see if they were affected. Finally, we went outside to see if the power outage affected other homes in the neighbourhood. To our amazement, warm lights emanated from other residents' windows except ours.

Moving into our new home was an exciting prospect, but unfortunately, our confidence and happiness were quickly shattered due to the lack of light. This experience in May 2023 reminded me of the early 1970s in the UK when many companies operated under a 3-day week due to the rationing of electricity caused by the fear of coal shortage[1].

Consumed with confusion and "amygdala hijack", I quickly dialled the Scottish Energy supplier. However, we were assured that the power cut would be restored by the morning and advised to go back to sleep.

By 6 AM, our curiosity grew by thousands out of proportion as no light was in sight. Our fridge freezer began to shed tears of water as the ice melted in response to our present crisis.

Immediately, one of our neighbours knocked on our front door to ask if we had light. Then, and only then, we realised that they, too, woke up in the early hours without a power supply.

A phone call I made attracted everyone outside our property. In this instance, I called John Smith, the Site Manager who supervised the construction of our new home, to tell him of our situation. John was a remarkable leader known for his unwavering sense of Purpose.

He promptly departed from his residence and drove straight to our street. John earned widespread respect for his ability to lead, ignite change, and enable people to realise their full potential. He assured us that he would resolve the power outage issue with Scottish Energy. With unwavering courage, John, as always, led us through our darkest moments, empowering residents to find their strength within.

"I can't promise anything if I know I wouldn't fulfil my promise."

I'm passionate about John Smith because he's 'the Man With Purpose'. *"I don't promise* [homeowners of] *anything if I know I wouldn't fulfil my promise,"* is the statement I heard direct from John in one of my conversations about his leadership styles.

This man has an uncanny ability to ignite a spark within others, especially during adversity. No wonder John received many accolades and won numerous awards and bonuses from his employer.

By July 2023, John's company recognised him with numerous awards for his exceptional leadership, teamwork, client engagement, and resilience in the building industry. John's framed photograph is now proudly hung on the walls of the company's prestigious headquarters in Edinburgh, Scotland, as a mark of honour.

John Smith demonstrated how true leaders function even in odd times in leadership - be it in families, businesses or relationships. A leader with a clear sense of Purpose shares this vision with their team, uniting them behind a common goal. Purpose serves as a guiding light, illuminating the path towards greatness.

In addition to fostering collaboration, Purpose cultivates Trust. Trust produces a culture of shared beliefs and values through which the individual or organisation lives.

The Essence of Purpose

At its core, Purpose is the synthesis of one's passions, talents, and values. It is the authentic expression of what truly matters to an individual. Purpose goes beyond prestige, fame, and material wealth, delving into the depths of who we are as human beings. It is the profound conviction that our existence has a higher meaning and that our actions can contribute to a greater good.

Clear Vision and Goals: The Critical Factor for Growth

Having a 'Purpose' alone is not enough. 'Purpose' must be coupled with a clear vision and tangible goals. An image or a mental picture serves as the lighthouse in the storm, providing a beacon of direction even during the darkest times.

Purpose clarifies the path forward, ensuring that every action aligns with the original intent. Alongside a vision, leaders must set up SMARTER goals as enablers to progress steadily, providing a sense of achievement and fulfilment.

When Purpose, vision, and goals intertwine, they create powerful growth catalysts. They ignite the inner fire within leaders, pushing them to uncover their full potential. Challenges become Steppingstones. Failures transform into invaluable lessons. And obstacles become mere opportunities for growth.

In conclusion, it's crucial to remember that the Power of Purpose can influence both leaders and followers, transforming entire organisations. When leaders embody and communicate their Purpose, it permeates throughout the whole structure, aligning each member towards a unified mission. John Smith's spark was not just a symbol of light in the dark but represented the collective Power ignited by a leader driven by Purpose.

As leaders in your organisation, you must embrace your inner fire, nourish it with Purpose, and share its brilliance with others. Only when you find the courage to ignite sparks in others, especially in the hearts of people outside your inner circle, can you guide and empower them to do the same and illuminate the world with purposeful leadership.

Chapter 2 Exercises: The Power of PURPOSE in LEADERSHIP

Exercise 1: Personal Purpose Reflection:

(1a) Reflect on your values, passions, and goals to discover your Purpose as a leader, manager, or employee.

....

....

(1b) Discuss with a mentor or a coach how aligning your Purpose with your leadership can enhance your effectiveness.

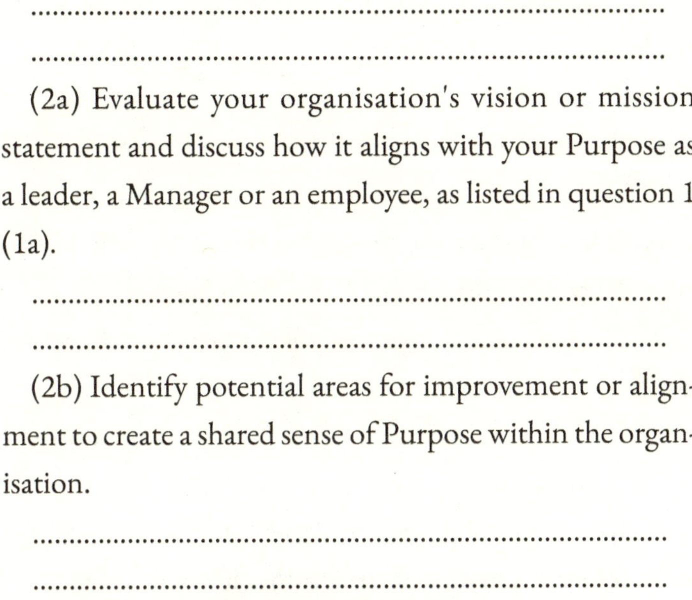

....

....

(2a) Evaluate your organisation's vision or mission statement and discuss how it aligns with your Purpose as a leader, a Manager or an employee, as listed in question 1 (1a).

....

....

(2b) Identify potential areas for improvement or alignment to create a shared sense of Purpose within the organisation.

....

....

Exercise 3: Purposeful Goal-Setting

DO NOT set SMART Goals, but set **S-M-A-R-T-E-R** Goals to align with Purpose and organisational vision. Track your progress and evaluate how aligning your goals with your Purpose improves your leadership effectiveness.

Using the S-M-A-R-T-E-R goals listed below, complete the goals you have set this week, this month, or this year and how they align with your Purpose and the organisation's vision.

S: Specific KPIs (key performance indicators): This answers the questions of "What, Where, When, Which, and Why" is the project necessary at this time and not next year?

M: Measurable KPMs (Key Performance Metrics): Are the KPIs measured in value: ££, $$, quantity in hours (how many?), or other units?

A: Achievable: Can you achieve the task within the available budget?

R: Relevant: Is it the mission and vision of the organism? What value does it yield, and 'Who' benefits from it?

T: Time-bound: How long will it take us to achieve the goals?

E: Evaluate Progress: Check KPMs against initial S-Goals and t-times, and review accordingly.

R: Re-adjust the processes: Amend the SOPs and, possibly, set up a system so it runs with auto-pilot.

Write your **S-M-A-R-T-E-R** Goal statement here: (e.g ., I want to pay off my mortgage in the next three years by working two jobs).

....

....

Exercise 4: Purpose Communication

(4a) Develop a communication plan to effectively articulate the Purpose and vision of your organisation or team to stakeholders.

....

....

(4b) Practice delivering clear, compelling messages that inspire and motivate others to align with the Purpose.

....

....

Exercise 5: Purpose Activation

(5a) Take "Action" by starting projects or initiatives that directly contribute to your Purpose as a leader and the organisation's vision.

....

....

(5b) Reflect on the impact of purpose-driven actions on your leadership style and the overall performance of your team or organisation.

....

....

The upcoming Chapter will guide you to unleashing The Power of Identity in Leadership. You will discover and comprehend your self-worth, empowering you to lead confidently, establish authentic relationships, and positively impact everyone around you. I am confident that this will be a transformative experience for you.

---

1. Kingsley, Thomas (Dec. 2022): 'Tedious and horrible': What life was like during the 1970s blackouts;https://www.independent.co.uk/news/uk/home-news/scheduled-blackouts-uk-1970s-life-b2245675.html [accessed on 22 August 2023), Independent Newspapers.

Chapter Three

The Power of Identity in Leadership

Embracing Your True Self Through Reflection

Many years ago, a man who attended one of my training programmes in Manchester, England, once stood at the edge of a vast mountain range. The wind whispered through his hair as he gazed at the horizon. I was curious about finding out why he attended our leadership academy. During our conversion, I understood that this man was born into a family with a long lineage of successful business leaders and had always felt the weight of expectations from others pressing upon him. He had dropped out of college to join his father's business empire in Birmingham.

Everybody in his neighbourhood assumed this man would follow in his father's footsteps, continuing the family's legacy of wealth and influence. But within himself, he felt lonely, disconnected, and unfulfilled.

As he stood there, feeling the crisp mountain air filling his lungs, he realised his true calling lay elsewhere: Motivational Speaking.

In this moment of self-discovery, surrounded by nature's raw beauty, this man reflected on his journey toward self-awareness and authentic leadership. His journey towards self-awareness began when he took a leap of faith and decided to forge his path in the Motivational Speaking Business. So, he wanted to develop himself through one of our business training programmes.

He delved deep into introspection, questioning his desires and passions in life. As he continued his self-exploration, he found inspiration in the stories of others from different industries - in business and politics - who had embraced their true selves and achieved remarkable success.

In the business world, two prominent individuals stood out for this man: Satya Nadella, the CEO of Microsoft, and Oprah Winfrey, a media proprietor, author, television producer, and American talk show host. Why? Because Nadella had defied expectations and brought a fresh perspective to the tech giant, transforming the company into a global powerhouse. On the other hand, Oprah Winfrey has unapologetic authenticity and dedication to uplifting other people, making her an internationally renowned media mogul.

In the political landscape, a notable political leader whose ideas align well with his beliefs about identity in leadership is Jacinda Ardern, a former politician and the 40th Prime Minister of New Zealand (2017-2023). He chose Jacinda because of her demonstrated strength and compassion during times of crisis, leading her country with empathy and resilience. *"It takes courage and strength to be an empathetic and compassionate leader,"*[1] she said.

With these inspiring examples listed above, he felt a renewed sense of Purpose as he embraced his leadership Identity - the unique combination of strengths, values, and experiences that defined who he is. The mountains echoed his determination as he vowed to use his unique strengths and values to impact the world through Public Speaking positively.

I cited this man's story, not because of his privileged background or dropping out of college, but because this story illustrates one's journey to self-discovery, self-development, and the realisation of the transformative Power of Identity. It's about embracing one's individuality to become an impactful leader in their own right. He didn't want the glory of his father's name to overshadow his natural gifts, even though his career choice might conflict with his family's background.

Five Steps for Cultivating Leadership Identity

With extensive training and several opportunities to speak publicly across the globe, I have acquired five invaluable pieces of knowledge on cultivating leadership identity within organizations.

Step #1: Embracing the Soul of Leadership

To become an exceptional leader, one must first embrace the soul of leadership. It means recognizing one's unique qualities that make one a great leader. Embracing this essence unlocks the potential to inspire and motivate others. The genuine desire to positively impact others starts with compassion, empathy, and empathetic behaviours. Embracing and nurturing this soul of leadership leads to a remarkable journey of self-discovery and growth.

Step #2: Understanding Identity in Leadership

Leadership comes from within and relies on understanding your identity. Reflect on your values, strengths, and passions to shape your unique leadership style. Recognize that self-awareness and self-improvement are ongoing processes. Aligning your identity with leadership unleashes your full potential and creates a strong foundation for success.

Step #3: Be Part of the Transformative Journey

Creating lasting impact and transforming others are the hallmarks of leadership, which extends beyond personal accomplishments. To lead a transformative journey, one must possess a clear vision and Purpose. It's imperative to articulate a compelling vision that inspires others to achieve greatness.

You become an influential change agent by sharing this vision and empowering individuals to be their best selves. Being part of this journey affirms your leadership identity, as you enable others to unlock their potential with confidence and determination.

Step #4: Be Authentic and Real!

My most outstanding leadership mentor, Dr Myles Munroe (1954-2014), consistently described the term' authentic Leadership' as 'True Leadership'. In this paragraph, I would use "True Leadership." To truly lead with impact, it is imperative that you embody genuineness, trust-building, and consistency. Consistently upholding your values makes those around you feel secure and empowered to reach their full potential.

True leaders share their vulnerabilities, allowing those they lead to connect with them on a deeper level, leading to enhanced engagement and commitment.

Leaders must confront their beliefs, biases, and prejudices while pursuing true leadership. They learn to embrace diversity, inclusion, and the Power of different perspectives.

They recognize the importance of building teams encompassing a wide range of experiences, thoughts, and backgrounds, harnessing the strength that diversity brings.

Remember, displaying these traits is not optional, but essential for effective leadership.

Step #5: Developing a Personal Ethos

Developing a distinct personal ethos is essential to your leadership identity. It requires introspection and aligning your moral compass with your leadership style, empowering you to make principled decisions in challenging circumstances. Your core values and beliefs form the foundation of your ethos, enabling you to be a confident and effective leader.

In conclusion, leadership identity is a multifaceted concept, encapsulating an individual's values, experiences, and future aspirations. Embracing a strong leadership identity is a transformative journey that requires embracing the soul of leadership, understanding your concept of identity in leadership, being part of the transformative journey, and developing a personal ethos.

By mastering the five steps outlined in this Chapter, one can become a truly exceptional leader capable of inspiring others and effecting positive change. This process enables one to stand out as a confident and influential leader capable of driving progress and making a lasting impact.

It is essential to embrace one's leadership identity and unlock one's true potential to achieve this level of success. The world eagerly awaits the exceptional leadership that such mastery can bring.

Chapter 3 Exercises: The Power of identity in leadership

(3a) Self-Reflection and Personal Values:

Take some time to identify your core values and personal beliefs and write them down. Consider how these values and beliefs shape your identity as a leader and guide your decision-making. Share your findings with others and discuss how your values align with or differ from their own.

....

....

(3b) Conduct a 360-DEGREE Assessment:

Ask colleagues, superiors, and subordinates for feedback on your leadership style and characteristics. Analyse the responses to identify themes and patterns contributing to your leadership identity. Create an action plan to strengthen positive aspects and address any areas of improvement.

....

....

(3c) Strengths and Weaknesses Assessment:

Evaluate your leadership strengths and weaknesses. List five key strengths contributing to your leadership effectiveness and identify three weaknesses you want to improve upon. Create an action plan to address these weaknesses.

....

....

(3d) Seek out Diverse Perspectives:

Step out of your comfort zone and engage with individuals who have different backgrounds, experiences, and viewpoints from your own. By actively listening and learning from others, you can challenge your own identity as a leader and broaden your perspectives.

....

....

(3e) Create Leadership Storytelling and Mission Statement:

Craft a mission statement that captures your Purpose, values, and aspirations as a leader. Continuously revisit and refine this statement as you grow and evolve. Share it with your team to foster alignment and guide collective efforts.

....

....

---

1. Locke, Suzzane (Jan 19, 2023), 'Jacinda Ardern: 8 quotes that prove her #inclusiveleadership.' (20https://aurora50.com/jacinda-ardern-8-quotes-inclusive-leadership/ [accessed 22 Aug. 2023]

Chapter Four

The Power of INSIGHT in Leadership

Expanding the Boundaries

In business and leadership, insight means recognising and understanding others (their emotions and feelings), perspectives of others (stakeholders), market dynamics, customer preferences, industry regulations, and cultural differences.

Recognising your personal weaknesses is crucial for leadership growth. Exploring your areas of self-improvement can open up new opportunities, just as Emmanuel discovered through his epiphany below.

Emmanuel's Uncharted Path: An Epiphany

Emmanuel, a remarkable young boy, lived in a small town in the heart of a rural area Ozizza, Afikpo, in Ebonyi State LGA of Nigeria in West Africa. After completing his first school year, he followed in his parents' footsteps and became a fisherman, farmer, and carpenter to avoid being labelled a street urchin with no future direction.

With the help of sponsorships from his eldest brother, Sir Charles Amadi, Emmanuel returned to formal education. He saw education as the key to changing his life circumstances and was determined to forge a new path.

From Secondary School to the prestigious University of Nigeria, Nsukka, Emmanuel earned distinction in his first degree. After a few years of hospital practice training and serving in the mandatory Nigerian National Youth Service Corps (NYSC), Emmanuel won a full-time scholarship from the Ebonyi State Government in 2002 to study for his Master's degree in the United Kingdom.

As if that was not sufficient, Emmanuel obtained a postgraduate Diploma from the University of Brighton (UK), an Executive MBA (Lancaster University Management School, UK), MBA Master Class, 'Doing Business in China' – with distinction at the Guanghua School of Management, Peking University, Beijing, China (May 2011) and a Doctor of Philosopher (PhD) degree (Dec 2019) (UK).

His Professional development saw him attend some of the world's prestigious universities, including the Executive Education programme of the Cass Business School, City, University of London (9 May 2018) (renamed as Bayes Business School), and Harvard University Extension School (11-12 Sep 2019) - to keep himself relevant in this dynamic changing world.

Between London and Northwest England, especially in North Manchester, Emmanuel had a stint as a Manager across various Business Multiples in his profession for many years. He worked diligently at this company, steadily refining his skills on the corporate ladder. His outstanding work ethic and ability to inspire others were always admired.

However, he felt that the "bosses" and "practice managers" were not effectively and efficiently resolving staff and business issues, creating red tape that subjected him to ticking boxes. He also felt that a 'special ingredient' was missing from his leadership style - an intangible quality that would enable him to make a difference truly. Little did he know that his journey and curiosity towards this realisation would lead him down an uncharted path, where INSIGHT would become his most valuable asset.

In 2009, Emmanuel took the bold step and resigned from his managerial post to study for an Executive MBA to understand what goes on 'behind the scenes' - in the head versus the mind - of Senior managers and business leaders.

Since his graduation in 2011, Emmanuel has remained unemployed. Why? Because he found the secret through the corridors of education – his Executive MBA.

As an entrepreneur, he had set up several businesses and grew them from scratch to a profitable standard before packaging and selling them to emerging entrepreneurs.

By November 2019, he set up a Leadership Academy | Executive Education company to help Senior Managers, Sales executives, and stakeholders enhance their organisational performance – the poor performance he saw ten years back.

While walking through Boggart Hole Clough Park in Blackley, North Manchester, Emmanuel stumbled upon a group of children deeply engaged in a game of hide-and-seek. It struck him that a true leader not only understands the needs of their team members, but also cultivates a culture of Trust, empathy, and innovation, ultimately driving the team towards remarkable accomplishments.

Emmanuel's Leadership Lessons: "From the Unseen to the Seen"

There are five leadership lessons to learn from Emmanuel's Epiphany.

Lesson #1: The Necessity of Self-Reflection and Innermost Knowledge

Emmanuel soon discovered the necessity of self-reflection as a critical aspect of developing insight into leadership. He understood that by pausing and delving into his thoughts and emotions, he could better understand himself as a leader.

Through introspection, he uncovered his strengths and weaknesses, enabling him to align his actions with his values. Emmanuel realised that by clarifying his Purpose and communicating it passionately, he could inspire others to find their own and foster a culture of shared goals and aspirations within his team.

Lesson #2: Continuously Learning: The Path to Mastery

Emmanuel understood the significance of continuous learning in achieving leadership excellence. He proactively sought various opportunities to expand his knowledge and skills, including attending conferences, participating in workshops, reading, and exploring diverse perspectives. Until now, he has surrounded himself with over 100 leadership books to understand other authors' views on life.

With an unwavering commitment to lifelong learning, Emmanuel gained access to valuable insights and solutions that helped him navigate intricate challenges and motivate his team.

Lesson #3: Embrace Diverse Perspectives to Drive Innovation and Change

Emmanuel recognised the value of diverse perspectives in driving innovation and change. He fostered an inclusive environment where unique insights were encouraged, leading to unprecedented growth and success.

Lesson #4: The Power of Insight from Warren Buffet

Warren Buffet is a true champion of long-term thinking. He leverages his vast knowledge to inform his investment decisions, consistently evaluates risks, exercises independent thought, and remains a perpetual learner. It's no wonder he is widely acknowledged as a visionary leader.

(5) The Power of Insight: Jacqui Lambie - from Parliament to the Masses:

Jacqui Lambie, the Tasmanian Independent Senator, and founder of the Jacqui Lambie Network (JLN), is an exemplary leader who leverages her deep understanding of her constituents' needs and challenges to champion transformative policies. Her commitment to embracing diverse perspectives, continuous learning, and reflecting on her values and Purpose has earned her widespread influence.

Insight is an absolute necessity in leadership. Self-reflection, learning, and a wide range of perspectives drive innovation and change, propelling and inspiring others to make a profound and long-lasting impact.

Exceptional leaders like Warren Buffet and Jacqui Lambie are propelled by insight that drives positive change in the world.

Finally, remember that the 'Emmanuel' used in this illuminating anecdote is genuine and not fictitious. He's Dr Emmanuel Eni Amadi, the Founder & CEO of Amadi Global Leadership Academy | Executive Education, Glasgow, UK. He's the author of many books, including the one you're reading now: Unmasking the Power Within: Mastering The 5 Forces of Self-Awareness For Extraordinary Leadership.

Chapter 4 Exercise: The Power of insight in leadership

(4a) Practice Active Listening:

Engage in conversations with team members or colleagues, focusing on understanding their perspectives. Ask open-ended questions, summarise what they say, and avoid interrupting. Gain insights by valuing others' thoughts and opinions.

....

....

(4b) Conduct a SWOT analysis:

Evaluate your leadership strengths, weaknesses, opportunities, and threats. Reflect on how these factors impact your ability to lead effectively and identify areas for improvement.

....

....

(4c) Embrace curiosity and continuous learning:

Cultivate a growth mindset and seek opportunities within and outside your current discipline to expand your knowledge and skills. Attend conferences, read books or articles, and participate in workshops that enhance your understanding of leadership and management.

....

....

(4d) Seek Feedback from Diverse Sources:

Actively seek constructive feedback from different perspectives, including team members, peers, and superiors. Create a safe space for open communication, establishing regular touchpoints to receive honest feedback and gain valuable insights about your leadership effectiveness.

....

....

(4e) Practice Empathy:

Empathy is crucial for gaining insights into others' feelings and experiences. Make an effort to understand the challenges and emotions of those you lead. Through empathy, develop a deeper understanding of how your actions and decisions impact individuals and the organisation.

Chapter Five

The Power of Reputation in Leadership

Legacy Through Impact

'Reputation' refers to how others view an individual, group, or organisation. In leadership, reputation is crucial and built through ethical decision-making and inspiring actions. This Chapter examines how a leader's reputation impacts their success and legacy.

The Echoes of Impact

As we dive into the realm of impactful stories, one cannot overlook the fantastic tale of the Echoes of Impact. This story has been whispered among the IGBO-speaking generations in Eastern Nigeria in West Africa and ingrained in the annals of leadership history. It serves as a testament to the transformative Power of reputation.

Growing up as a teenager in West Africa, I was always the naughty one causing trouble at home - probably seeking attention. While my sister got her meal portions separately, Our mother usually served my elder brother and me food on a single plate.

I had always stood on the path of equality right from childhood. With a big plate of meals served on the table, I would always tell my brother to demarcate the meal, especially the meat: one portion is his, and the second is mine. When situations don't work in my favour, I remember throwing away a plate of soup out of anger when my brother broke our agreement.

When he reacted in self-defence, my action was to resort to a corner and 'cry me a river' for hours to garner sympathy from our mother.

There was this story my mother used to tell me about a 'King' and his 'Reputation' just to put a smile on my face in one of those angry moments.

Whether this story is a folktale passed to her by my grandmother or something she heard in the village, this story has been with me for nearly four decades. It was a story about a wise and virtuous king named "Eze Agu" of the IGBO tribe in ancient Biafra. When translated into English, that name means "The King of Lions". "Once upon a time, a King ruled the Kingdom. Throughout his reign, he became known for his unwavering moral compass, pursuit of justice, and empathy for his people. His reputation spread far and wide, reaching neighbouring kingdoms." She paused for a while and smiled. Then, she looked at me straight to establish eye contact before continuing with her tale. "His Kingdom was on the brink of war with Aro, but neighbouring kingdoms inspired by King Eze Agu's REPUTATION stepped forward to mediate peace talks.'

'The legacy of King Eze Agu extended beyond his lifetime, shaping his Kingdom through ethical leadership and decision-making that earned him a reputation of trust, integrity, and excellence.' He concluded before holding my hands to lift me.

The Eleven Proven Steps for Building a Leadership Reputation

To build a reputation worthy of a lasting legacy, I have identified eleven simple steps anyone can harness to make an excellent reputation across various industries. The first three steps will explore three critical steps from two renowned business leaders and one political figure who have left their marks on the world, including Jack Ma, Mary Barra, and Aung San Suu Kyi.

Step #1: WEAR YOUR VISION WITH CONSISTENCY

Jack Ma, the co-founder of Alibaba, is widely respected for his relentless pursuit of innovation and entrepreneurial spirit. He built his reputation by consistently inspiring his team to embrace out-of-the-box thinking and transform the e-commerce landscape.

Ma's leadership legacy lies in the fact that he revolutionised how businesses operate, leaving an indelible mark on the global e-commerce business community.

Step #2: Fall in Love With Ethical Decision-Making:

Mary Barra, the CEO of General Motors, represents another powerful example of reputation-driven leadership. Barra's reputation as a strong advocate for sustainability and forward-thinking decision-making allowed her to transform General Motors into a leader in electric vehicle technology. Her legacy will endure because she influenced the automotive industry, shaping its path towards a cleaner and more sustainable future.

Step #3: Inspire Others as if Your Life Depends on it:

The words "inspire" and "inspiration" have their roots in theology, meaning "to breathe into" or 'to breathe in'. According to the first book of Moses: *"And the Lord God breathed into' his nostrils the breath of life, and the man became a living being."*[1]

Therefore, when you *'inspire'* people under your charge or give them *'inspiration'* to achieve anything of value in their lives, according to the first book of Moses, you have given their lives meaning.

Aung San Suu Kyi, the State Counsellor of Myanmar akin to a Prime Minister, exemplifies the strength of one's reputation in catalysing transformation. Even while confined to house arrest for a prolonged period, she ardently championed the cause of democracy and human rights. Despite personal sacrifices, Suu Kyi's unwavering commitment to her principles made her an international symbol of freedom. Her leadership in fighting oppression and standing up for justice will inspire future generations.

Step #4: Define Your Core Values:

As a leader, it's important to identify and articulate your core values and personal beliefs. These values serve as a foundation for your reputation and guide decision-making within the organisation.

Step #5: Communicate Effectively:

Enhance your ability to communicate effectively and confidently to convey your vision, goals, and expectations. Effective communication is the key to fostering engagement and alignment.

Step #6: Cultivate Strong Relationships:

Establishing and maintaining strong relationships with coworkers, staff, and partners is essential. This will improve your standing as a leader and provide a support system.

Step #7: Encourage Collaboration:

Fostering collaboration and teamwork creates an inclusive environment that fosters innovation by encouraging diverse perspectives and ideas.

Step #8: Embrace Continuous Learning:

Invest in personal and professional development. Be a lifelong learner and adapt to new challenges.

Step #9: Take Calculated Risks:

Demonstrate your unwavering self-assurance and take assertive action by venturing beyond the boundaries of your familiar territory and embracing calculated risks.

Step #10: Deliver Rcsults:

Ensure you and your team maintain high standards. Keep your focus on achieving measurable outcomes and delivering consistent results that will undoubtedly create a positive impact.

Step #11: Design Your Exit to Leave a Legacy of Lasting Values:

In the context of leadership, planning one's exit may sound counterintuitive and counterproductive. After all, is it not the ability to remain in Power indefinitely the sign of a great leader?

Throughout history, wise leaders have consistently recognised the vital importance of preparing for the future by cultivating the next generation of leaders. Passing on the torch of leadership ensures a lasting legacy of triumph and is a powerful motivation for others to step up and lead with unwavering conviction.

By practising this, we impart valuable experience and knowledge to future generations, shaping a brighter future for all. Some compelling examples of this principle can be found in the following statements, *"It is for your benefit that I am going away. Unless I go away, the Advocate [the helper, the councillor, comforter, strengthener) will not come to you, but if I go, I will send Him to you."*[2]

Jacinda Adern, the ex-Prime Minister of New Zealand (2017-2023), understood the Power of Reputation in Leadership. She, too, knew that leaving her office and 'passing on' the baton of the premiership to new breeds of leaders is the secret to a lasting legacy.

When announcing her departure from office, she emphasised the responsibility that comes with a privileged role, stating, *"After six challenging years, I am leaving because with such a privileged role comes responsibility – the responsibility to know when you are the right person to lead and also when you are not."*[3]

These statements hold valuable insights for leaders seeking to create a lasting impact. As the leader of your organisation, it is vital to recognise the necessity of your departure for the next phase of your mission to unfold.

Leadership begins with mentoring. Stepping aside and introducing mentorship and empowerment programmes will allow young and emerging leaders to develop their leadership skills and carry on your legacy. They'll copy your legacy and use it as a standard reference for generations to come. Leaders cultivate talent, ensure smooth transitions, and create a lasting legacy transcending their tenure. As John C. Maxwell once said, *"A leader's lasting value is measured by succession."*[4]

Therefore, build a reputation that goes beyond individual achievements and creates a legacy of positive change by planning your exit simultaneously.

As we conclude this Chapter, let us be inspired by the transformational force of reputation, as demonstrated by leaders throughout history, such as King Eze Agu, Jack Ma, Mary Barra, and Aung San Suu Kyi.

By embracing the importance of reputation in leadership, we can build our legacies with confidence and determination. According to Lao Tzu, an ancient Chinese philosopher, *"A leader is best when people barely know he exists; when his work is done, his aim fulfilled, they will say: we did it ourselves."*[5]

Chapter 5 Exercises: The Power of Reputation in Leadership: Legacy Through Impact

(5a) Define your leadership values:

Clearly articulate your core leadership values and principles. Continuously reflect on how these values guide your decisions and actions. Ensure you consistently align with your stated values to build a reputation of integrity and authenticity.

....

....

(5b) Set meaningful goals:

Establish goals that align with your larger Purpose as a leader. Focus on creating a positive impact beyond short-term success. Regularly measure progress toward these goals and communicate your commitment to achieving them with your team and stakeholders.

....

....

(5c) Trust-Building Exercise:

Choose a colleague or team member and engage in a trust-building activity. This could involve sharing a personal story, delegating a task transparently, or seeking advice on a challenging situation. Reflect on this exercise's impact on your reputation as a trustworthy and reliable leader.

....

....

(5d) Seek opportunities for mentorship and coaching:

Engage in mentorship and coaching relationships to expand your knowledge, skills, and perspectives. Being mentored or coached by respected leaders in your community can provide valuable insights and support as you work toward leaving a lasting and positive impact on your organisation and community.

....

....

(5e) Continuously develop yourself as a leader:

Commit to lifelong learning and development. Keep up with emerging trends, best approach, and appropriate skills in your field. Seek opportunities to attend conferences, workshops, and training programs contributing to your leadership expertise. You can increase your impact and leave a lasting legacy by continuously growing.

....

....

(5f) Stakeholder Perception Assessment:

Identify critical stakeholders (colleagues, clients, subordinates, superiors) and gather feedback on their perception of your leadership reputation. Ask for both strengths and areas for improvement. Analyse the feedback and develop strategies to enhance your reputation where needed.

....

....

(5g) Conflict Resolution Simulation:

Participate in a conflict resolution simulation where you must navigate and resolve a complex conflict situation. Please pay attention to how your reputation as a leader influences the resolution process, and learn from it to improve your reputation management skills.

....

....

---

1. Gen 2:7 (emphasis placed here).

2. John 16:7 – (emphasis was added)

3. Locke, Suzanne (19 Jan. 2023): Jacinda Ardern: 8 quotes that prove her #inclusiveleadership. Source: [accessed 22 Aug. 2023]

4. Maxwell, John C. (1998 and 2007). The 21 Irrefutable Laws of Leadership (10th ed.), p.264 . Harper Collins Leadership, USA.

5. Shinagel, Michael (2013) "The Paradox of Leadership", Professional Development, Harvard Division of Continuing Education, Michael Shinagel Blog (3 July 2013): Available at: (accessed: 22 Aug. 2023).

Chapter Six

The Power of IMAGE vs BRAND in Leadership

In today's highly competitive and ever-changing world, leaders must recognise the significance of their Brand in shaping their leadership journey. *IMAGE* or *Brand* concept goes beyond logos and taglines; it encompasses an individual's reputation, values, and unique qualities.

The term *'IMAGE'* holds significant Power and influence over circumstances. 'Image' encompasses the perception and impression others have of the leaders and the organization's claimed identity, values, and culture. Therefore, 'Image' plays a crucial role in shaping their success.

When your Image or Brand is projected on billboards or screens in London, New York, or Sydney streets, it becomes the subject of public scrutiny. As a leader, your reputation is automatically exposed when people hear your name, see you on TV, or read about you on pages of newspapers. Therefore, you are as successful as your Image or imprint could be.

Through a notable example from the UK, USA, and theological perspective, we will delve into the Power of Image and its impact on business leadership.

'Image' in the Context of Theology

The term "image" was first introduced to the world by the Creator of the universe in the creation story. The statement goes like this: "*Let us make mankind in our own IMAGE, according to Our likeness*" (Gen 1:26).

This statement of authority is inherent in creativity – and generally refers to all humans being created 'godlike', but with limited qualities and characteristics that reflect the divine Creator. It demonstrates the creature's capacity to mirror the creator's supernatural attributes and display qualities such as love, justice, and mercy.

Let me clarify that the attributes and traits of specific actions and reactions generated by a particular product are instilled in creations by the Creator or manufacturer. Therefore, the minds of the individuals who create such products are reflected in their products - the Image. Any attribute not included during production cannot be anticipated in the product.

In like manner, the mindsets of the people (scientists, manufacturers) who developed the two American nuclear bombs that destroyed Japan's Hiroshima and Nagasaki in 1945, unfortunately, were as dangerous as the atomic bombs themselves.

IMAGE is also about creativity vs. innovation, rationality vs. responsibility, spirituality vs. morality, and the ability to have a relationship with the maker. That's why we have Business Relationship Management (BRM) in business. All luxury goods manufacturers will always want to establish long-term relationships with their customers through guarantees, warranties, and 'software' upgrades to maximise customers' experiences with their products.

Image vs. Brand
In the Context of Leadership and Business

When it comes to leadership and business, *Image* is a corporate responsibility. Corporate Image encompasses not only the actions and conducts of individuals and organizations but also the 'perception' of their Image and reputation. This perception, or mental picture, represents the impressions that members of the public hold as accurate for that individual or organization.

Therefore, *"Image"* encompasses reputation, credibility, and the overall impression they create through actions, values, and words (communication). A leader's Image is a crucial asset that can influence the behaviour, attitudes, and Trust of their partners in business, including employees, customers, shareholders, and the general public.

When relating this concept to leadership or business, it is essential to consider the implications our actions and interactions have on others. Every person has intrinsic value and deserves respect and dignity. This behaviour can shape ethical leadership and promote workplace fairness, equality, and empathy.

Recognising that humans can make choices, hold different opinions, exercise reasoning, and have a sense of Purpose can influence leadership styles that empower individuals, encourage personal growth, and provide opportunities for meaningful contributions.

Case Study: Sir Richard Branson - Virgin Group

Sir Richard Branson, the founder of Virgin Group, is a prominent example of a business leader who transformed a failing business into a global brand through the Power of Image or brand marketing.

Beginning as a music retailer in the early 1970s, Virgin struggled to compete against established players in the

UK market. However, Branson's visionary leadership and strategic emphasis on IMAGE propelled the Virgin Group to new heights. The story about this man is publicly available online. This man clearly understood the significance of IMAGE and branding in capturing the attention and loyalty of customers.

Branson created a brand that stood out from the crowd by projecting a rebellious and innovative IMAGE through unconventional marketing campaigns and stunts. His emphasis on IMAGE became the catalyst for Virgin's success across various industries.

TEN Strategies or Techniques for Developing Leadership Image vs. Brand

To develop a powerful leadership brand, leaders must follow proven strategic paths that align with their values and the desired influence. Below are ten steps I discovered to guide you on your journey towards building a solid leadership brand.

Step #1: Define Your Purpose:

Defining your Purpose is crucial in building a leadership brand. Understanding what drives you and what you hope to achieve as a leader allows you to communicate your vision effectively and attract others who share your values.

Clearly articulate your mission and values, highlighting what sets you apart. As discussed in Chapter 2, "Purpose is the alignment of your actions, wills, and intents to the original reason why you exist or something exists". 'Purpose' is the original intent of the maker, the essence of its existence, and why you wake up in the morning, grab your car key, hop in your car, and drive to work. Why? Because you feel a strong sense of fulfilment in your career as it perfectly aligns with your personal values and beliefs.

Step #2: Understand Your Audience or Market:

Identify and comprehend the needs, aspirations, and expectations of your target audience or followers. Understanding your audience is essential for effective leadership branding. By recognising the needs, expectations, and aspirations of those you lead, you can tailor your approach and effectively inspire and guide them toward a shared goal.

Step #3: Embody Authenticity:

Be genuine to yourself, aligning your actions with your values. Embodying authenticity is critical to building a strong leadership brand. Being true to yourself and expressing your values genuinely creates Trust and credibility. People are more likely to follow a leader who is genuine and consistent.

Step #4: Demonstrate Consistency:

Consistently exemplify your values and maintain a reliable presence to build Trust and credibility. Demonstrating consistency is essential for building a leadership brand. Consistency in your words, actions, and decisions builds Trust and establishes a reputation for reliability. People are more likely to trust and respect a leader they perceive as consistent.

Consistency is the foundation of character building, and your character makes room for success and to dine with kings and queens. Consistency breeds character. Character breeds Trust. And Trust generates true leadership. In the words of John C. Maxwell, one of the best authors on leadership, "*Your success stops where your character stops. You can never rise above the limitations of your character.*"[1]

Step #5. Communicate Effectively:

Craft a clear, captivating, and impactful message for your target audience using various communication channels. Effective communication is vital for leadership branding. Developing strong communication skills allows you to articulate your vision, inspire others, and motivate your team. Clear, concise, and compelling communication lets you connect with your audience and establish your leadership brand.

Step #6. Prioritise Integrity:

Be ethical and honest in all aspects of your leadership, demonstrating a commitment to integrity. Prioritising integrity is fundamental to leadership brand development.

From my research on the origin of the word, 'integrity,' – I discovered that the term we use today has its roots in French and Latin. In French, integrity is 'intégrité' (/ɛ̃.te .ɡʁi.te: pronounced as *anté-griti*), and in Latin, 'integers' ► "integritas". Both words mean the same: 'integer', 'intact', 'integrate', 'entirety', 'whole' or "one". That's why we are told that *"I and the Father are one."*[2] In other words, 'I and the Father,' the Source of Life, are one and in unity.

In Hebrew, I also understand that for humans, 1+1 = 2, whereas for the Creator of the universe, 1+1 =1 = Holy. In another setting, we heard this statement being utilised powerfully in the Scripture: "*Verily truly I tell you, the Son can do nothing by himself; he can only do* [publicly] *what he sees his father do* [secret behind the scenes]". The passage continues, "*.. because whatever the 'Father' does, the 'Son' also does.*"[3]

To become a leader, a manager, or an employee with integrity, whatever you do in secret (= 1) should be a replica of what you do or say in the public domain (=1). Whatever opinions you hold about yourself or others on the outside should be the 'replica', the 'entirety', the 'one' and 'wholeness' of the same values and beliefs you hold deeply inside – in the secret chambers of your mind.

Upholding integrity requires strict adherence to moral and ethical standards, honesty, and consistently acting with your values. Integrity means standing by your beliefs and values even in the face of challenging times. By aligning integrity with your leadership brand, you build Trust and establish yourself as a person of character.

Step #7. Cultivate Relationships:

Building genuine connections with others and fostering a sense of community and collaboration are essential for leadership branding.

Making meaningful connections creates a network of support, credibility, and influence. Nurturing relationships helps foster collaboration, loyalty, and amplification of your leadership brand.

Step #8. Embrace Vulnerability:

Embracing vulnerability is an essential aspect of leadership branding. Being open, transparent, and willing to show vulnerability fosters connection and Trust. It communicates that you are human and approachable, which can inspire loyalty and commitment in your team. You can show vulnerability by sharing personal stories and experiences, allowing others to connect with you more deeply.

Step #9: Continuously Develop Yourself:

Continuous personal development is vital for building a leadership brand. Investing in your growth and learning demonstrates your commitment to ongoing improvement and inspires others to do the same. Building expertise and staying current in your field enhances your leadership brand.

Step #10. Leave a Legacy:

Leaving a legacy is a concept that cannot be underestimated and is the ultimate goal of leadership branding. Strive to create a positive, lasting impact on those you lead, the organisation or community you serve, and the world. By leaving a legacy, you solidify your leadership brand and inspire future generations of leaders. Envision the impact you want to make and work towards leaving a positive and lasting gift.

These ten steps serve as a roadmap for leaders to develop a strong leadership brand. By following these principles, leaders can establish Trust, gain influence, and leave a lasting impact on their teams, organisations, and communities.

A prime example of a leader who successfully built a trusted leadership brand is Barack Obama, the 44th President of the United States.

Building a strong leadership brand requires dedication, self-reflection, and a commitment to upholding one's values. Obama paved the way for genuine influence and impact by focusing on integrity and establishing Trust.

As we conclude this Chapter, may leaders and emerging leaders be inspired to reflect on their Brand and embrace the opportunity to build a trusted legacy that shapes the future.

Chapter 6 Exercises:
The Power of Image vs. Brand in Leadership

(6a) Perform an Image / Brand Audit:

Evaluate your current personal Image vs. Brand as a leader. Analyse how others perceive you and compare it to how you want to be perceived. Identify areas where your Image could be strengthened or adjusted to align with your leadership goals.

....

....

(6b) Develop a Personal BRAND statement:

Craft a concise and compelling statement describing who you are as a leader and your value. Use this statement consistently across various professional platforms and communications to strengthen your Brand.

....

....

(6c) Use Social Media strategically:

Utilise social media platforms like LinkedIn, Instagram, and Facebook to their fullest potential and showcase your leadership abilities to advance your professional career. Regularly contribute to relevant online discussions and share thought leadership.

....

....

(6d) Image vs. Brand Consistency Exercise:

Evaluate how you consistently communicate and embody your leadership brand across different platforms and interactions. Review your emails, social media profiles, and public speaking engagements to ensure consistent messaging and brand representation. Make adjustments as necessary to maintain a strong and cohesive leadership brand.

....

....

(6e) Network Strategically:

Build a network of professional connections to help elevate your Image vs Brand. Attend industry events, join professional associations, and engage with online communities to expand your reach and build valuable relationships.

....

....

(6f) Thought Leadership Initiative:

Please select a topic within your industry and develop a thought leadership initiative. Write articles, give presentations, or host webinars to demonstrate your expertise and reinforce your leadership image vs. Brand as an industry influencer.

....

....

(6g) Practice Assertive Communication:

Practice assertiveness to improve your communication skills. It would be best to convey your ideas, expectations, and thoughts confidently and respectfully. Seek opportunities to practice assertive communication in both professional and personal settings.

....

....

1. Maxwell, John C. (1998 and 2007). "The Law of Solid Ground: Lesson 6 from The 21 Irrefutable Laws of Leadership", pp. 61-71; Harper Collins Leadership.

2. John 9:30 (NIV)

3. John 15:19 (with emphasis added).

Conclusion:

The Unveiling of Greatness

"Unmasking the Power Within: Mastering the 5 Forces of Self-Awareness For Extraordinary Leadership" comprehensively explores the various dimensions of Power in leadership. It unravels the potential within leaders, inspiring them to embrace their true selves, ignite their Purpose, build a trusted brand, gain unique insights, and leave an enduring legacy, thus transforming themselves and the world around them.

Examining these forces, "Unmasking The Power Within" creates a framework for leaders to develop a deep understanding of themselves and their impact on the global landscape.

Chapter 1 delved into the concept of Power in leadership, emphasising the need for leaders to recognize, understand, and embrace their hidden Power to lead others effectively.

In Chapter 2, we explored the Power of Purpose in leadership, highlighting the importance of having a clear vision and sense of direction. Leaders can inspire and motivate others by aligning their actions with their Purpose.

Moving forward to Chapter 3, we discussed the Power of IDENTITY in leadership, emphasising the significance of self-awareness and authenticity. Understanding one's values, strengths, and weaknesses allows leaders to connect with others and build Trust effectively.

Chapter 4 focused on the Power of INSIGHT in leadership, highlighting the need for continuous learning and reflection. By cultivating insight, leaders gain a deeper understanding of themselves and the world around them, enabling them to make informed decisions.

In Chapter 5, the book uncovered the Power of REPUTATION in leadership, emphasising the long-term impact of consistent actions and behaviours.

Finally, in Chapter 6, we explored the Power of *Image* vs. *Brand* in leadership, highlighting the need for leaders to understand and cultivate their Brand. Leaders can influence perceptions and generate Trust and credibility by effectively managing their IMAGE vs.aximize Brand.

In conclusion, "Unmasking the Power Within" presents a holistic approach to leadership, incorporating the dimensions of Power discussed in each Chapter. By mastering these forces of self-awareness, leaders can profoundly impact the Global Landscape.

APPEAL FOR WEEKLY ACTION:

I acknowledge that "Unmasking the Power Within" is not a quick-fix solution. Instead, this book is a comprehensive guide that empowers individuals to traverse their leadership journeys with authenticity, resilience, and impact.

By unmasking the often hidden and untapped Power within, leaders can elevate themselves and those around them, creating a ripple effect that extends far beyond their immediate spheres of influence.

To apply what you've studied in this book and improve your ability to influence others to follow you, I implore you to take the following actions:

1. Embrace your Power in leadership and recognize its potential for positive influence.

2. Identify and define your Purpose as a leader, creating a sharp vision and sense of direction.

3. Cultivate self-awareness and authenticity, understanding your values, strengths, and weaknesses.

4. Continuously seek insight through learning and reflection, gaining a deeper understanding of yourself and your world.

5. Focus on developing a solid reputation through consistent actions and behaviours

6. Build and maintain a positive image through effective communication and perception management.

7. Finally, actively manage your Brand, leveraging it to create Trust and credibility.

By taking action on these seven points, you can integrate the concepts and strategies in the book into your daily leadership practices, to unlock your full potential as an impactful leader. With open doors, you will attract a world of infinite possibilities and become a person of influence in your job, profession, and workplace.

About the Author

Dr. Emmanuel Eni Amadi (PhD, MBA, MSc, PGDip, B.Pharm) holds a Doctor of Philosophy (PhD) in Medical Sciences from the University of Bradford, England, UK (Dec. 2019) with special interests in Pulmonary Nanotoxicology, Graphene Oxide Nanoparticles, DNA Damage in Lung Cancer, COPD, and asthma patients.

He's a Harvard-trained Strategic Leadership and Emotional Intelligence consultant and a prolific author of three books. His professional Development programmes saw him attend some of the world's best Business Schools, including Cass Business School, now known as Bayes Business School, City, University of London; Guanghua School of Management, Peking University, Beijing, China, and Harvard University Extension School, Cambridge, USA. He is an invited speaker at some of the world's Nanotoxicology Conferences.

As the Founder & CEO of Amadi Global Leadership Academy | Executive Education in Glasgow, Scotland, United Kingdom, Dr Amadi mentors senior managers through his professional development company at www.amadiglobal.co.uk.

Previously, Dr Amadi served on several School Governing Boards as a Non-Executive Director/Board Trustee, including The Oak Learning Partnership - a Multi-Academy Trust (MAT) in Bury, Greater Manchester, and as a School Governor at St. John Bosco R.C. Primary School, Manchester, UK where he provided strategic oversight to the Heads of the Schools.

He's passionate about the science of human emotions and their influence on thoughts and leadership. His research has focused on self-discovery and self-development to uncover the secrets to success not typically taught in the classroom. As a result, he published "Emotional Rulership" in 2022 and "Unmasking The Power Within" in 2023 to help others succeed in Life.

The Amadi's family, consisting of Dr Emmanuel Eni Amadi and his wife, Mrs Ewa [Eva] Amadi, with their two teenage sons Michael (14) and Anthony (12), moved from England to the City of Glasgow, Scotland in 2023 to raise up the next generation.

Books Published By The Author

https://www.amadiglobal.co.uk/publishing

How to Contact us

To partner with us, participate in one of our executive leadership training programmes or to buy this title in bulk quantities for special sales order for your corporate training, branding or electronic versions, please visit us at:

Amadi Global Publishing
An imprint of Amadi Global Leadership Academy
Executive Education
The Global Centre
Glasgow, United Kingdom

www.AmadiGlobal.co.uk
info@AmadiGlobal.co.uk

www.ingramcontent.com/pod-product-compliance
Lightning Source LLC
LaVergne TN
LVHW090123160826
845673LV00015B/830

* 9 7 8 1 7 3 9 8 7 7 8 2 8 *